There's lots to laud in *Harmony River*, Stephen Jaech's new poetry collection, but what engages me most is Jaech's willingness to proffer an abundance of sensorial detail. In these expansive poems, the reader gets to "press a hand to the wound," smell "wet wool and Bay Rum," hear a goldfinch "thump against the window," taste "silver salmon splayed and dripping fat into the flame." *In Harmony River,* the reader doesn't spectate; s/he participates.

-**Michael Darcher, Author of** *Odd Comfort* **and** *The Silver State Stories*

Conifers, water, rocky landscape, and low light inhabit the outer and inner worlds of a Pacific Northwest poet. Stephen Jaech's long-awaited collection has all that and more with "confluences, waves/ and wind channeling us/ on our brief passage." *Harmony River* views with empathy and subtle wisdom the moments that make up that passage. Attention to the movement of words mirrors attention to details of environment and seasons. But grace and beauty can overlay pain—and life is full of pain in all its forms. Where there is loss or pain, however, there is also redemption found glancingly in a slant of light or the daily changes of "Today, a sweet magnolia, tomorrow a field of snow." With apologies to Stephen, who is a private person, I must use this line from "The Gift of Music" to sum up the book: "the wonder comes out/ from the trembling of his heart."

-**Sherry Rind**, *The Storehouse of Wonder and Astonishment* **and** *Between States of Matter*

It took me two or three days to get past the first poem in Steve Jaech's gem lode of a book. First, because the poem was a knock-out punch. Then, I had to sit back and absorb, to read random lines and savor parts of the original experience. Finally, I just wanted to read again and live the poem. "It is/ an unlatched gate you enter and find/ a recognizable cobblestone path/ and a familiar porch where you/ are always welcome and where/ the door opens before you knock." So it is with *Harmony River*: enter and live.

-**James Cervantes, author of** *From Mr. Bondo's Unshared Life* **and** *Sleepwalker's Songs: New & Selected Poems*

harmony river

ISBN 979-8-9903358-1-3
Library of Congress Number 2024918798

Pleasure Boat Studio: A Nonprofit Literary Press
pleasureboatstudio.com
Seattle, Washington

Cover art by Raewyn Harris
Art P. 46-47 by Bill Rades
Cover and book design by Lauren Grosskopf

for
Kathrina, Kris, Stephanie, and Jiayun

Stephen Jaech is grateful to the editors
of the following publications where
some of these poems first appeared.

Poetry Northwest
College English
Porch
Christian Science Monitor
Seattle Review
Four Zoas Press

Harmony
River

Poems by
STEPHEN JAECH

 Pleasure Boat Studio: A Nonprofit Literary Press

Contents

I.

II.

III.

IV.

V.

I.

Enduring Grace

Before words appeared on vellum,
before moonlight shone on river

ripples, before hoofprints tamped
tracks on mudflats where deltas

adjoined seas, even before chants
rose from clans squatting

near driftwood bonfires, it lay
dormant like bone marrow stem

cells in the flesh of all that is
or ever was. Natural as plainsong

it lifts up voices as celebrants
congregate, and here on carved

sandstone or rendered in wood,
or infused in stained glass,

or trembling on the lip of a bronze
bell, it arises as surely as an oozing

spring, newfound as a hatchling
cracking its shell. In lullabies

from mother's mouth it soothes
an infant's cry. Vital as air, it

combs through our hair.
In dreams and in choir lofts,

resonances stunning and rare.
Yes, it is a comrade long dead

who shows up one day, rings
the doorbell as you fall to your

knees while the sky turns
like a Lazy Susan, and you ask,

"How can this be? My friend,
how can this be?" Nothing refutes

reason more than to see that face
you kissed, your friend long dead,

to know he's returned to you.
It is a drink of ice water in the shade

of the ramada. It is peaceful slumber
near a warm hearth. It is an embrace

when you are sick at heart. It is
an unlatched gate you enter and find

a recognizable cobblestone path
and a familiar porch where you

are always welcome and where
the door opens before you knock.

Point of Light

"In a dark time, the eye begins to see..."
—Theodore Roethke

Is it near or far afield
that point of light across
the way? We strive

upon solid ground as we
aim toward all we see,
the only focal point burning

a hole through obscurity.
We move with purpose
on frozen soil, yet that sole

light remains remote,
out of reach. Our shadows
merge with a vast darkness

that shrouds the gap between us
and that point of light, now
no closer, nor brighter

than it was before.
When we close our eyes,
radiance reigns emblazoned

against an awning of space
there where water, earth,
and sky meet the eye.

Hoisting Flowers

Don't we ponder
what follows elevating

rituals that uphold us,
ones ushering us

to hallowed places?
When spring insists,

flowers ascend
and bees return.

Extending a vase lifter,
I hoist sweet peas

and baby's breath
to the mausoleum's

top row. The long pole
shivers as the gray plastic

budvase clicks into its notch.
These wispy flowers tremble

against the marble wall.
Looking toward them,

I whisper to my parents,
raising my face as I did

when I was an infant and
they stooped to lift me up.

Sound of Wings

Startled by wings, I thrill to see the sky
tumbling in birds, thousands falling
like a black veil where willows stoop
to touch the shore. Birds in sync, a wall

of them, then more, countless more,
they twitter and peep, a skein whirring
over the lake. Their fluttering, their tremors
ripple, a shuffling pall within a winter stirring.

Who can explain what brings them here
on the coldest day of the year? Climbing a stair
of light, they again stir, a waking dream, there
to rise and send a wraith arrowing through the air.

These tiny hearts beating haste against grief,
their wings shuffling in a clamor so brief.

Voice Within

A bulge bursting at its seam,
a word slithery as an eel,
I know it's there inside, unseen.

A mole worming beneath the green,
clawing along a darkling hall,
a bulge bursting at its seam.

A seed in a pod, a rock in a stream,
it dwells like a clapper in a bell,
I know it's there inside, unseen.

An ant entombed in amber resin,
a weeping child in an abandoned well,
a bulge bursting at its seam.

It comes to light and falls back again,
a palpable pulse that cracks a seal,
I know it's there inside, unseen.

A moan, a laugh gagged and weaned
on walls of an anchorite's cell,
a bulge bursting at its seam,
I know it's there inside, unseen.

A Field of Snow

When he steps from the porch and walks
through an open gate, the sky unfurls forever.
Beneath the sweet magnolia, he talks

to fluttering crows above a field of snow.
The morning star overarches a frozen lake.
Shall today be a sweet magnolia, he wonders,

and tomorrow a field of snow? He'll make
hope an open gate and fear a covered well.
A neatly made bed, a wicker cradle in the shed —

what to make of these? Light floods through
the cellar door, shaping what is there and what
is not, suffusing all the way words do. For joy

we paint the front door red. We zing
rocks across a frozen lake. We tell no one
why we line the mantelshelf with portraits

of our smiling dead. All history shall
become a burn barrel and now, this minute,
lives as a sawing flame. Love, a morning star,

hope an open gate. Beyond the garden
hedge, a forest, dark and cold. Today,
a sweet magnolia, tomorrow a field of snow.

II.

A Good Story

gnashes conflict and has a mercurial
plot that zigzags like an EKG line.
Mystery, too—why does a rabbi weep
at the backdoor. Hey, whose blood blots

this antimacassar? Do I hear footsteps
in the sealed attic? A child's cry rises
from the mouth of a deserted well.
A good story has characters that one feels

like stubble on a jawline, and one may sense
their leaving by a hint of cigarette smoke
suspended in parlor air. A good story will keep
one off guard: 4 a.m., a brick shatters the kitchen

window, the phone rings and rings as lights
flicker, and the Weimaraner whimpers
and trembles beneath the bed. A good story
will recoil, withdraw, finally, like a garter snake

sliding through a hole in a garden wall.
A good story clangs and clangs: a steeple bell
tolling at midnight, waking the townsfolk
who, in their nightwear, fill the square.

Oh, yes, a good story returns like the cat
one grieves over and buries, the cat matted
in dirt, the one that claws open its grave
and now yowls loudly at the screen door.

Creative Process

The avant-garde artist screws bone to bone,
splices flesh to flesh, sculpting the living thing.
An electrical storm sparks the lub-dub heart
that begins, begins, begins again, and again

to fuel muscles, tissues, and zippered adhesions.
While the torpid creation twitches, resurrecting
on a tabletop slab, magnesium light racks castle
mansards and floods the mountaintop. Amazed,

the creator weeps as his incarnate design heaves
against restraints and snaps its anchored chains.
How could one know that this reanimation would
disobey its artificer, would stagger into the village

where an angry mob gathers with pitchforks
and torches to encounter what they refuse
to countenance? Reshaped in body and blood,
the hapless miscreation sobs as it slouches

over fields and swales. Breathing fiercely,
alone, it thrashes through tangled thickets,
bereft of hearth and history. Its unfamiliar
hands club boughs and wildwood that lash

its bleeding face. Delving into a wilderness
where rotted roots poke through forest loam,
it stumbles and howls for some recognizable
space, for a shred of ineffably shattered meaning.

Stalker

Wherever I go, she tags along.
Habitually hiding in my blind spot,
she's a presence at my back.

You may have noticed her tattered
coat, graceless gait, clubfoot scraping
the pavement. That paralytic face

taunts me, one jowl droops, a string
of spittle dangling like snot. Her lips
barely move when she talks, scarcely

a recognizable word. I tell the cops,
but they say, "Our hands are tied."
Come, come, you must have noticed her,

whiffed her wet wool scent, and felt
her elbow nudge you as you waited
at the curb for the light to turn. Her

freakish reflection floats in the shop
window as I mutter curses over my
shoulder. When I wake from night

terrors, I sense she is in the closet,
or maybe kneeling at the door,
her one good eye at the keyhole.

She whispers augural oaths and limps
through the house while I sleep.
When I dream, she hagrides me,

her dirty fingernails gouging my back
as she squeezes my breath away.
Mornings, her scent lingers in bedsheets,

her fishy odor fouling my skin and hair.
She drapes herself upon my shoulders,
slithery lips licking my ears. When I

glance in the mirror, she vanishes.
She inhabits me, though, a symbiont.
Trying to ditch her, I kickstart my Harley,

pipes popping, and thunder up the hill.
But I feel her clinging to my back and hear
her hair flapping like a starched flag.

Getting There

You arrive at an unfamiliar depot
in an unfamiliar town, don't
understand the language, and have

no money. You can't identify
placenames on the wall map that
other travelers consult, so you ask,

"Where am I?" The stationmaster
must have called in sick, the hands
on the clock don't move, and bathrooms

are bolted shut. You approach
a uniformed man, an officer perhaps.
"Excuse me, sir, do you speak English?"

His eyes widen and he grips his cudgel,
shouts words that strike like fists, so
you jostle through the crowd, hurry

over blacktop roads until you approach
a circus tent in a horseless pasture,
red pennants fluttering. You have no

ticket, but a carnie ushers you to a front
row seat next to a clown. As whipcracks
pop, the ringmaster flourishes wild gestures

toward acrobats who tumble over barrels,
and then the elephant parade precedes
a dwarf riding a donkey. Perhaps you

suffer delirium, so you ask the clown,
"This is a funny daydream, right?" You
get no answer. The audience applauds

when a geek thrusts a sword down his
throat. Oh, and the ringmaster waves
melodramatically and points to a procession

of freaks. The audience stands and stomps
their feet. You notice a bearded woman,
a girl who has snakeskin, a man who twists

his head backwards through his legs,
a hunchback leading a two-headed goat,
and a boy with claws for hands. As trapeze

artists soar, you drain your voice shouting,
"Bravo, Bravo!" Nearby a lion roars while
a woman does a handstand on a galloping

white stallion. The clown begins to howl.
You feel like weeping. After the human
cannonball, Icarus the amazing midget, flies

overhead, you see flashing lights and breathe
in sulfurous smoke. At that moment, you
realize that you have never been so happy.

Hostage

Day and night, I hear him moan
for rescue, stomping on the attic

floor, my ceiling, scuffling his chains
across planks that separate us, his howls

stirring my broken slumber. It's what
he deserves, son-of-a-bitch always

whining about one thing or another.
I've chained him to a load bearing post

that supports the whole house from falling
into itself. Daily I send him cold leftovers,

franks and beans via the dumbwaiter,
sometimes a jug of tap water. For sure,

it stinks up there because the coal
bucket I left him must be full of slops.

When I removed his blindfold, I kicked
him in the face. Son-of-a-bitch bled

on my leather Doc Martens, too. I may
kill him, starve him to death, not send

a ransom note. I don't need the money.
His suffering gives me pleasure. Routinely,

I take a mop handle and thump the ceiling
while screaming, "Nobody loves you,

you son-of-a-bitch, so just die." But that's
a lie. I will climb the ladder for atonement.

I'll whisper, "I'm sorry, you son-of-a-bitch,
so sorry." Sure, I admit it. Probably I'll

start bawling and beg for forgiveness
as I lug him downstairs and tuck him

in my king bed. Yeah, sure, I confess.
I love the son-of-a-bitch like a brother.

Flying Friends

While crickets' chirp, I climb
a switchback that ends at a clearing
where silhouettes in wingless
flight sail on thermal currents.

Circling like hawks, they soar,
fugitives whom I knew so well
sliding along aisles of air. Each year
more appear banking on breezes.

As meadow grasses rustle, my path
vanishes in creeping thyme. Lingering
near a stony ridge, I look up at their
ascendancy as they turn and turn.

Like suction on a loose tooth,
an updraft bears me toward them.
Their tender draw I resist, as one
might refuse a kite's pull and shiver.

This leaf-littered autumn I reach
their spectral roosts where a lowering
sky bleeds through spruce limbs.
Still they hover so near. I know

I stand in failing light, and my unsure
gait pauses where tracks meet dizzying
dark. Even so, a frisson draws me
home once again, to familiar fences,

to whinnies of horses, to a porch
light glowing through mist, to banks
of blackberries drying on their vines.
Remembrances, though, flutter above

and soar over the barn, wheeling
and swerving as they come and go,
these deserters who dart and hang
in crevices of air, forever, forever there.

III.

Dark Houses

We arrive at an abandoned town and stand
before dark houses — horsetails pry through
concrete, blackberry brambles overflow

gray fences. We move cautiously, fearing
the sorrows we may find among sagging porches
and floors softened with dry rot. Fastened

to concertina wire circling the collapsed
courthouse, a red-lettered sign: "No Entry."
Hollowed-out façades, tumbledown marquees —

swallows flutter from beneath decayed eaves.
Public Park, too, has gone wild, long grasses
overwhelm the amphitheater, pavilion blackened

by fire. We pause near a steel chain attached
to a dog collar, articulated bones and yellowing
skull strewn in a trampled circle of dirt.

Wilderness annexes the playground. Where are
the children? Didn't we see a curtain flutter,
clapboard house, "No Trespassing" sign fixed

to the garden gate? Didn't we detect roasting
chicken aromas waft over a laurel hedge?
Who binds sweet pea vines to the trellis?

Someone must live here, a caretaker who sees us
pause near the shuttered armory. Evenings, we
hear coyotes scream and caterwauling in dim alleys.

Ahead roads lead to places renown for festivals
and wine, but we shall stay here among broken
houses and neglected gardens. We shall mend

rooftops and stairwells, search cellars and carry
flaming torches. We shall sweep glass shards
from windowsills and whisper prayers, bruising

our hands as we dislodge heavy stones, our legs
cramping as we stoop into small spaces. So many
dark houses. Liens on lives, liens on these platted

streets, we sort unopened mail, faded photographs,
and wire clothes hangers strewn on closet floors.
At the fourth wall, we strain to hear the slightest

sound. We kick open stuck doors. We enter
a sunlit room, hearthstone still warm. So many
rooms. So many dark houses. Someone lives here.

Wandering

Leaving the cinder footpath
that borders Saint Simeon Psychiatric

Hospital, I tramp across the county
park and cut through a horseless pasture

where a crippled colt named Cy
used to greet me, heave his head

and whinny when I approached.
Beyond the pasture fence, I enter

a ravine where coyotes hunt jackrabbits
at dusk and where I once stood petrified

at the sight of a black rat snake basking
on a sunbaked stone. Near the dry creek

bed, I turn onto a deer trail that leads
to a gully where sedges grow and where

Lady Ferns flourish near a spring,
water oozing among limestone slabs.

Wedging through a thicket of saplings,
I enfold myself into a stand of trembling

aspens. Daylight dims. All directions
become trackless: dark, threatening,

lovely. Suddenly, I sense a shadow
moving inexorably closer, drawing near,

advancing within a few feet of me
while I hold my breath, anticipating.

I lean forward to perceive what may appear.
I open wide my arms. I open my arms.

To the Motorcyclist Going 140 MPH

"No!" I scream as you open
the throttle and shoot between

cars, silvery helmet bending low
over handlebars, knees hugging

the chassis. In racing leathers,
you zigzag through traffic

south of milepost 252. We see you
later on eleven o'clock news, Eye-

in-the-Sky exclusive from Chopper
Seven — rural road, roadblock ahead,

a half-dozen cruisers chasing, light
bars flashing. How you jumped

safely from your still running bike,
we will never know, but we witness

you sprinting across a pasture,
Belgian Malinois overtaking you,

wresting your arm, bringing you
down as troopers converge. Is it

disregard for limits, for circling
clock hands, that stimulates us

as we speed along thoroughfares
and veer onto exits we had not

planned on taking? Closing ground,
a conclusion doggedly pursues

us and will bring us down no matter
what we do. In the rearview mirror,

we see it gaining on us, and, as we
know, it is closer than it appears.

Making Faces

Beneath the loft's skylight, the artist leans
over his drafting table. A beehive kiln
glows nearby. He opens molds and reveals

fresh faces. Surely, you've seen him strolling
in the park or ascending stairs to his studio.
From my room below, I hear him move,

a door opening and closing, water knocking
through pipes, and clack-clack as he fashions
lacquered masks. I have seen him sketching

clouds and sunrays near the park wading
pool, children kneeling near his easel.
I have watched him ply his rasp and calipers

to sculpt a nose, an ear. I search the reflection
in my grimy window, but the light isn't right.
Where my face should be, I find a shadow.

Mysteries shroud what lies beyond light,
for all I see is dark relief of mountain peaks
forever silhouetted beneath a dawning moon.

Perhaps all days that ever were and that ever
will be have settled within that graying radiance
beyond the square. Yet I must say, I have heard

him sobbing when he recognized the beauty
he found propped onto the drying rack.
I can't help myself, I have listened at his door,

eyeballed him through the keyhole, and watched
his shadow bend toward the firebox's roar and glow.
As I linger on the ground floor, he slides wet clay

into the kiln, images amalgamating to create
new faces, images that harden and become this life,
these eyes, this smile, this tongue, these words.

The Gift of Music

Doesn't he just show up one day? Some say he fell
from the sky. Others say he washed up from the sea.
But most say he is one of us who came from nearby.

Yeah, he serves food and drink, an' his grace sinks
into our bones. An' he says, "I'll show you" an' touches
our lips, an' then starts to make what he means.

An' he blows the sound of the horn. An' then he strains
the strings tight an' makes them cry. An' then he
        stretches
some skin right over the kettle an' beats something fierce.

An' when he opens his mouth, the wonder comes out
from the trembling of his heart. Like a blown open door,
out it all comes. Yeah, out comes the will-o'-the-wisp.

Out darts the frog's tongue. Out comes breeze in the
        boughs.
Out come silver coins. Out spills moonlight.
Out comes a curl of smoke. Out comes rain on the roof.

Out comes the black butterfly. Out comes the dove's coo.
Out come the groan and the kiss. Out comes firefly glow.
Out comes the blue scream. Out comes worn out shoes.

Doesn't he just show up one day? Maybe he fell
from the sky, or maybe he washed up from the sea,
or perhaps he is one of us who comes from nearby?

Deep Darkness Grows Darker

End of a rural road, close to an abandoned
cowshed, I duck through a gap in barbed

wire and walk across windswept fields.
On grazing land, miles from city lights

and ballparks, beyond up-lit billboards,
I merge with a pasture and a sweep of sky.

Dusk descends, darkness growing darker still.
I drift across rutted ground and whirl

among stars, stars. Traveling across open
space, I lift my eyes to an immense arc.

How could I know clouds would eclipse
all light as if I had no sight? How could I

know when to turn, where to go in darkness
so deep I could not see my own feet?

Then, by surprise, another creature comes near.
I sense its presence: a rustle of air, a soughing

of breath, and a silhouette subsuming me. It looms
close and terrifies me, as I reach out to touch it.

IV.

Pass the Potatoes

He sits at the head of the table
as if time stopped fifty years ago
and now pauses in the kitchen

as we say our dinner's grace.
Father asks how our day has gone.
"Your mother needs some help

with the dishes after supper," he says.
"But Mom is dead," I say. "She left
us twenty years after you died, remember?"

He takes a moment to digest the fact
before he says, "Son, have some yourself,
and then pass those mashed spuds this way."

Panegyric

To pay tribute, I spoke no lie as I
addressed mourners. Had you been
there, you would, I'm sure, have found
my anecdotes apt. Folks grinned, some

laughed quietly, others daubed a tear,
so, all in all, the eulogy went well.
Just now, though, I recall touching
your cool forehead as you lay dying.

As a parting gift, you gave me
a Krugerrand that I keep in a safe-deposit
box with a shell casing your color guard
handed me after the committal—a coin,

a shell locked in a bank vault. Why,
I wonder, do I often replay that instant
from our youth? You at the wheel
of your pink and white '56 Ford Victoria,

windows rolled down as we drove far
beyond city limits, girlfriends leaning
on our shoulders? Later we stopped
at a lookout above a ceaseless, dark sea.

Dead Drivers

Father, I noticed you drove by the house.
Our two-tone, teal and white, 1955 Chevy

Bel Air cruised down the street, and I
caught a glimpse of you as you turned

the corner, so why you didn't stop and say
howdy? Come to think, I marvel at how

many cars cruising by are driven by blithe
folks whose funerals I attended. Harold

freewheeled by in his Nash Metropolitan,
the one he died in when he got T-boned.

He squinted at me like he always used to do.
Oh, by the way, what was Grampa doing

in a WW II Jeep? He didn't have a driver's
license, did he? Still, there he was smoking

that meerschaum pipe and honking his horn
as I stood stunned, as if history's catacombs

had cracked open and a herd triceratopses
bolted down the street. Tell the truth, I'm

gobsmacked. Remember old man Zandt,
corner grocer, stumpy bald guy who always

sat on a stool behind the dirty magazine rack?
Well, Dad, I saw him, too. He came by riding

a Harley Screamin' Eagle. He pulled up
to the curb and started jawing, but I couldn't

understand a word because the bike's exhaust
pipes popped and rattled. Not only that,

but his Stahlhelm covered his forehead, so,
well, he looked ridiculous, like a hatchling.

After a while, he headed up the hill, engine
blasting and doing a death-or-glory wheelie

like he was hellbent on killing himself all
over again. Didn't he cut his carotid and bleed

out in a hot bath? Dad, next time you take a ride,
pull over, roll down the window and talk to me,

for God's sake. I have lots of questions. I don't
know where to begin. How's Mom? I mean,

is she with you? Where have you been? When
you drive by and turn the corner, where are you

going? Odd thing, I drove by our old house, forty
years vacant, and the pussy willow, the one Mom

planted by the garden gate, was blooming
out of season. I almost wept because I thought

about the times I stood at that gate, waited
for you to come home, for you to ease the Chevy

to the curb. Love, fear, love, fear—when you
came home without seeing me standing there.

For You

I have turned this clay,
made this bowl,
my son.

I have mended this kite
that will fly
in any breeze,
my son.

I have lit torches
in the garden where you
may walk safely at night,
my son.

I have carried this heavy
stone,
my son.

What My Father Paints

For loneliness he paints a waiting room,
a sagging barn, shadows draping
an empty bed, a hillside of stumps.

For satisfaction he sketches a white
picket fence, a rooster on a roof,
the fat sail of a passing sloop.

For divination he fashions
a tunnel of trees, a shooting star
creasing the desert sky, the swoop
of a gull, and a blood moon rising
over a tropical lagoon.

For hygge he strokes a bonfire,
firewood on a grate, a reddish curl
of a peony shoot pushing
through loam, and a cupboard lined
with canned peaches and pears.

For sanctuary he draws a sheltered harbor,
stone jetties, tiny townspeople
without lips or hats or laughter or tears.

For love, for love he renders an open gate,
a freshly tilled field, harnesses draped
on a paddock post, and pastel
hills bursting into bloom.

For aspiration he squeezes
oil paints onto a palette
and spreads them, impasto
against drum-taut canvas,
creating gesso icefields,
opened windows to wide vistas —
blood-red, violet, robin egg blue —
tranquil countryside tracts.
He constructs rustic cottages
above whitewater rivers
and unfurls twilight that fills hollows
and settles across country lanes.

He creates small figures
at the far end of a golden field,
miniature people whose faces
we cannot see and who turn
toward a vast horizon.

These tiny lives,
one must admit, are
almost not there at all.

Hearing Footsteps

Over my shoulder, I sense an unsettling
pause, like a held breath — instinct alerting

me that someone draws near though I see
no one here. No one at the front door

either, for rarely does anyone knock other
than the Jehovah's Witness lady who asks

if I "have heard the good news?" I often
sense a presence approaching, a stirred

space redolent with the scents of wet
wool and Bay Rum. Summertime, I hear

dry grass crunching underfoot, so turning
to greet whomever steps forward, I find

I am pitifully alone. Caught in a moment
of mischief and poised to unmask this teaser,

I turn a corner, duck into an alley and hide
behind a fortress of dumpsters. I marvel

to find my late father, sangfroid as always,
beetling toward me. Wearing his OshKosh

B'gosh striped overalls and those paint-
spattered boots he regularly wore while

gardening after church, he comes near,
says, "Son, quit hiding and stand up straight.

V.

Woman Found in the Trunk of My Father's '55 Chevrolet Bel Aire

Dad prayed over Edith's remains,
her name written here in black
indelible ink on a duct tape cincture.
She's in this can which once contained

Hormel Chili with Beans. The crematorium
desiccated her before a mortician sieved
her pulverized bones into this can.
I found her rolling around in the Chevy's

trunk. Wedged between the spare tire
and snow chains, she had been stuck
there for years. My father had planned
to deliver Edith's ashes to an estranged

daughter, but Dad died before completing
his pastoral tasks. To my surprise, I found
Edith as I searched for a jack and lug
wrench, but then I recalled the story

Dad told when he lay in a hospital bed,
a story of a ceremony no one attended,
not an usher nor an organist. Dad recited
liturgy and made the sign of the cross

for Edith. No one there to mourn her,
not even a bystander. So, father, I now
think of those who left wanting a farewell
kiss, of Ruth weeping in a cornfield,

and of Amelia trying to circle the world.
More, I think of the dispossessed hidden
in dark anonymity, those overlooked
and abandoned as the latch clicked shut.

Insane Asylum Cemetery: Brick 1045

Last September, summer drought,
a grassfire scorched the cemetery,
clinker brick markers charred.

The registered patients identified
by chiseled numbers, though others
unknown, not even one stone,

merely concave lengths of blackened grass.
Poplars fringe 3000 niches. Brick 1045,
nearly effaced, worn by wind, fire,

rain, and decades of neglect,
lies among anonymous patients who
form lines in evenly spaced rational rows.

Face of God

Bubbling from the volcano's
throat, red-orange ejecta
and molten rock plumps

as magma blossoms and folds
creating a new landscape.
And yet. No recognizable

face forms, not in thunderheads,
not in sunsets, not in constellations.
Look to the ceiling: Michelangelo's

depiction of a bearded creator
floats aloft like a zeppelin
and points a finger toward

a lounging Adam. More, see
here, jejune paintings in museum
galleries, two-dimensional images

of an aging divine, windswept
hair and flowing robes,
lightning bolts firing

from his fingertips. Why do
we need avatars.? Look there
what comes from woodland

shadows, what countenances
us. A deer in the clearing locks
eyes on us. Innately lifting

its head in a slow, graceful
motion like a ballerina's arm,
it regards us with continuous

focus, observing us, transfixed,
foreseeing everything we are,
innocence and grace taking us in.

Hula Dancer

While the Pacific rocks, the dancer minces
small steps back and fore, back and fore.
Pinching sand between her toes, she sways

in synchrony with palm fronds. Her eyes
follow her hands, musical notes climb
a scale, her fingers riffling leaves of air.

Back and fore, back and fore, she stretches
for something beyond reach, her fingers
gliding birds, touch and go, touch and go,

again, once more. Back and fore, back
and fore, her hips circle her feet—surf
crashes to shore, clouds driving west

as everything moves back and fore,
back and fore. Hips, palms, sea, she
—back and fore, back and fore.

Other Side of the Door

This atrium swallows sound.
Scuffed by generations of foot-
steps, the oak flooring reflects
a tinge of pewter light winnowing

through a frosted glass transom,
crescent moon, above an ironwood
door. What's on the other side?
One wonders who joined joists

and beams? Who set the headers,
dovetailed wall to wall, and carved
fleur-de-lis on mahogany wainscoting?
So smooth this solid brass doorknob,

burnished and cool as river stone.
If one leans against the jamb, ear
flush to winding woodgrain, perhaps
the wind's whisper, water dripping,

a footfall, anything at all. And
yet, nothing. Jiggling the knob
slowly, grasping, twisting, and, uh,
not even a teeny budge. Locked.

No key. If only a slit of light
would reveal itself when one kicks
and pummels the door, but no hint
of what's there manifests itself.

Anybody there? Anyone? Eyeball
to keyhole, what does one foresee?
Perhaps an arcade leads to a door
similar to this solid, palpable door,

which may open to a river of starlight,
above a courtyard, to a colonnade
leading to a chateau with many rooms,
many doors, the other side of this door.

OCD

Did I, did I, lock the door,
lock the door? I did, I did.
Did I turn the knob, turn it twice?
Did I, did I count my steps?
Did I count my steps? If
I did, did I miss a step or two?

Did my heart skip a beat or two,
skip a beat when I tried the door,
tried the door? If I did, if
I tried the door, tried the door, didn't
I take two steps, two steps,
one-two one-two, one-two twice?

Did I turn off the stove, check it twice?
Did I, did I check it twice? Is twice too
much? No it isn't, no it's not! I took steps
to double-check the locks, latch the door.
Yes, I did. Yes, I did. Of course I did,
didn't I? Deadbolt and latch, if

one lock doesn't work, the other will. If
I test them — check them twice —
the house is locked because didn't
I say I checked them twice, one-two?
I always try the door, try the door.
Check it twice. Stepping

outside, I count each step, each step
on the riverwalk, starting again if
I think bad thoughts. When outdoors,
I smile at trees, smile once or twice,
because trees can read my thoughts, one-two.
Bad thoughts enter my head, did

I say? I turn them away, don't
I, as I start over, one-two. Each step
I count, one-two, one-two.
Did I lock the door, did I? And if
I did, did I try the doorknob twice?
I did, didn't I, turn the latch, try the door?

I did, I did, try the door, didn't I, didn't
I? Checked it twice, traced my steps.
Why do I, why I do what I do, one-two?

VI.

Harmony River

Here breathes Harmony River.

Here I wade through ankle-deep
riffles near the pebbled shore of Harmony River.

Here I cast a silver lure
into the slow-moving current
of Harmony River.

Here I feel a yank and tug
as a Coho salmon strips
line and roils the surface
waters of Harmony River.

Here a circling osprey
holds the breeze like a kite
above the gentle flow
that slides downriver
on glacial waters of Harmony River.

Here I wade hip-deep
across the mirror of the sky
as the fish heads upriver
with my silver lure in its red
mouth through the gunmetal
gray waters of Harmony River.

Here a logjam ruffles
the current near where I brace
against the pull that sweeps
downriver where the thrashing
fish fights to spit the barbed hook
of my silver lure in the numbing
waters of Harmony River.

Here the salmon leaps and wrests
to break free near the logjam
where I wade in a constellation
of backwash blebs while I tighten
the drag and raise the pulsing rod tip
above the whirling waters
that spin where I wade
in the swelling force of Harmony River.

Here whitewater boils
over river rocks and the silver
salmon's silhouette approaches
me as I brace myself in a current
wet with river-rush my rod beating
like a heart as the breeze soughs
through the treetops while my silver spoon
flashes in the milk of the rolling waters
of Harmony River.

Here I hoist the fish onto the low bank
its gills pumping bellows opening and closing,
its body bucking against the sharp air
its dorsal fin splayed in spasms of distress
and its scales flashing sequins

against dying sunlight as it fights
for life while I thread a wire stringer
through its mouth and gills and heave
the fish high over dancing
reflections glinting off Harmony River.

Here on the high bank I start a fire
with twigs and dry moss as I look
upstream where the moon climbs
over the spot in the shallows where
I had cast my line below the logjam
that now fades into a cool awning
of shadows and here I offer small
fir limbs and chunks of decaying
lichen-covered bark to the growing flames
that shoot embers sailing like fireflies
above the darkening waters of Harmony River.

Here bats loop and weave through a shaft
of smoke that climbs like a spout to a sky
speckled in stars as the moon plows
a furrow of light down the center of the river
now a soundscape of deep-toned frogs rasping
and croaking their throats to a din that floods
the river's hollow where a chill takes the shape
of river fog coiling along the bank and reaching
under the cedars and willows where the
            smoldering fire
sears the silver salmon splayed and dripping fat
            into the flame
as a night loon wails downriver and makes a tremolo
warble that splits the evening over Harmony River.

In the Garden Maze

In the garden maze
boxwood hedges channel us
toward a concealed center.
Turning and turning, we move

through boxwood hedgerows —
left, right, or straight ahead —
turning and turning, we choose
one lane or another.

Left, right, or straight ahead?
Mind you, we do not know which way
to go — one path or another.
A voice in the tower directs us,

for we do not know the way.
When evening settles on the garden,
a voice in the tower ushers us
through the darkening labyrinth.

Evening lowers its awning on us
within the garden and the maze,
so we depart the dimming labyrinth
to the lawn where we entered.

A garden surrounds the maze,
as we pause near the entrance
on the lawn where we started.
Birdsong fills the evening air

while we pause near the entrance,
rapt between here and there.
Birdsong chimes the evening air
as Venus rises from the sea.

Rapt between here and there,
we walk down a sloping lawn
as Venus rises from the sea
above the garden and the maze.

Garden Maze Caretaker

Your attention please if you move
with purpose the outing will stimulate
you one way in one way out do not
presume a pattern use your instincts
and recognize that your sightline
is blocked over the top and around
corners of the hedges more than likely
an open space awaits perhaps an alcove
where you may rest briefly on a garden
bench and contemplate which pathway
to choose next of course naturally
nothing is promised not even food
and drink I am obliged to inform you
that once you enter resist impatience
and anger need I say that damaging
hedgerows is forbidden if the journey
grows tedious you will annoy everyone
if you complain and please understand
no one will feel sorry for you so be
single-minded wits razor-sharp reject
timidity and take decisive steps while
enjoying the pleasure of being lost
the challenge of finding your way
free forgive me but I am instructed
to read these final provisos "this is
not a game if you are injured expect
no aid if you lose hope expect no
comfort if you remain in the maze
overnight do not move impulsively

in darkness" understand by the way
you should know that once you've
exited the puzzle you will find
yourself somewhere around here
I'm told perhaps on the other side
of the garden near the old orchard
before you choose which way to go
you must accept nothing is promised
even when you reach the maze's center
you will not know unquestionably that
your journey has finished and you may
ponder what you should do and what
will happen if you do nothing know
the advice from management always
has been to keep moving always keep
moving and to trust that where you
go is where you are meant to be

A Poem Crashes Against My Window
—One Thing Leads to Another

How can I help but wish for the fervid
flame of a burning bush, an inspiration

to lift me like smoke above the garden's
geometrics? In a trance, I stare at the blank

monitor when a thump against the window
brings me to my feet. Having banged

headfirst into my dormer pane, a goldfinch
lies motionless on cedar mulch. Eyeing

the hapless bird, I ponder how abruptly
life falls away to compost. A moment later,

though, the finch twitches, wriggles its head
and blinks its BB eyes, as if trying to find

its bearings. Will it recover? As I mull
over that question, I recall times when I

reveled beyond moderation and awoke,
unsure of hour or place, on an unfamiliar

couch. I recall sirens coming for Grandpa
after he collided against the French doors

on his way to the garden trellis where
wisteria blooms lured him to a shady spot

within a fragrant zone. Just now I come
again to my window. The finch is gone. Did

a hawk or a feral cat carry it off? A feather
about the size of an eyelash is all that remains.

I think of those stopped short en route
from one desire to another, lives hurrying

through sunlight when a hard knock forestalls
all plans. The sky flips upside-down, inside-out

—circle of light narrows, then squeezes shut—
blackout shades flapping like ravens' wings.

Music Makes Us Weep

Sunshine inflames the stained glass
while the boys' choir lifts Handel's

Hallelujah chorus to the doomed ceiling—
we stand, chins up—cyclonic harmonies

stir our fenced tracts, shearing
off roof tiles, recasting who we are,

who we wish we were. Composure
unhitching, we ascend, sweeping

above spires and steeples. With effort,
we try to deny sentiment but are overcome

as we mount sea swells that toss us
upon foreign shores. Why, we wonder,

shouldn't we fall to our knees, surrender
to jubilation? Don't sealed doors fling

open as the storm heightens, our wind-
whipped flags popping and snapping?

Takeoff power hurtles us down a dark
runway. Burdens abandoned, cabin lights

flickering, we rise above ourselves—now
and again now. The stained glass darkens

as we touch-down, hearts juddering.
Eyes still prickling, we leave oak pews,

and feel lighter, forgiven, and strangely
healed, as if cleansed in moving waters.

VII.

Curtains and Veils

Cattle graze in long shadows as we ascend
switchbacks to a headland concealed in fog.

At journey's crest, our trek reaches an arbor
leading to a tiled courtyard. We have no

money, no shoes. Watchful, one after another,
we file through portals, echoes resounding

in atria and along dark corridors, stone dust
and rainwater scents rising like hoarfrost.

Luggage gone, we gather in pavilions, vast spaces,
and stand close to each other, among others.

We have lost our clothes, our teeth. Our doors
are curtains, and our walls become veils that stir

as we move one after another. Curtains and veils,
sheer as dragonfly wings, brush our faces. Open

spaces become stanzas that ripple as we feel our
way one queue after another. Then yet another.

Forgotten lyrics return like communion wafers placed
on our unfurled tongues. When the conductor raises

the baton, we get ready while others approach
coming without end from moonless passageways

to stand in tiers among us and to join our harmony.
How could we know such a place exists? We wonder

who wrote these lyrics? And who, we wonder, who
is that clapping fortissimo on the unlit balcony?

Subjunctive Case

If you were to drive into town
to visit your estranged family
whom you have steered clear

of for 25 years, likely you'd
stop at the beanery to ask if Sen-
Sen is still for sale. Maybe you'd

drive down that rutted side street
where the Craftsman Foursquare
stood, now a vacant lot, knee-

deep wild grass, cobbled walkway
and cement rubble all that remains.
Maybe you'd ask around. Neighbor

says that house burned down 15
years ago. "Everyone died." You
ask, "Everyone?" You reckon

that your family may have moved.
Maybe they bought that houseboat
on Lake Union they always wanted.

If only you had kept in touch, maybe
you would not find yourself pacing
a circle round ashes where the rose

garden once grew. Maybe you will
leave town without visiting friends.
Maybe you will refuse to scream

or pound the steering wheel with
your fists. Rather, you probably
turn the car radio volume on full

blast. Maybe you're afraid to endure
this one-stoplight town, clapboards
sagging, pavement cracked. Maybe

you'll pull into a rest stop and weep
like a whipped orphan. Maybe you
will. Maybe you won't. If you were

to confess your trespasses, maybe
you'd stomp on the pedal and make
the engine roar. If you were to glance

in the rearview mirror because you
think you hear a siren, you'd be
stunned to find the high-pitched

screech originates inside your throat,
something clawing the cauterized hurt
that begins to breathe and bleed again.

Dying on My Feet

Prepared to write about the well-arranged bowl
of fruit that reminds him of a church lady's hat,
he considers the fleshy shapes, globes of Red
Delicious apples, hm-mmm, overripe bananas,

and plums swelling their skins, while the radio
ushers in the Twelfth Street Birmingham Revival —
beseeching the audience to be heard, as loud
as the radio goes. Bishop Malachi says he's seen,

hallelujah, yes sir, he's seen storm clouds
in the sky over Alabama. He says the time
is coming like thunderheads over Alabama,
yes sir. We'll be on our knees, he says, yes sir.

We'll drop to our knees, hallelujah, he says.
Do you feel the Holy Spirit, hm-mmm, in your
bones? Do you to hear the horses, the horses
in the sky? Do you hear them hooves? Yes, sir,

horsemen gallop in the skies over Alabama.
And drums thump, hallelujah, yes sir,
and I want you to know, hm-mmm, that swords
those horsemen swing will cut you down.

Yes sir, only one way to salvation, can I
hear you say, yeah, is down on your knees.
The way to make it home is to shout hallelujah,
yes sir, shout hallelujah and raise your hands

for one of them blue robes, yes sir, because
them horses in the sky over Alabama don't
trample them blue robes, no they don't, yes sir.
Let's hear you shout hallelujah for them

blue robes. You hear the drums beat
hallelujah? Come to the still waters
while drums pound hallelujah. Amen.
Yes sir, we'll float downriver which flows

into the gulf which surges into the ocean
which rises to the sky, the sky over Alabama
which blends into the Milky Way, can I
hear you say, which opens to the glass domes

of paradise, yes sir. The hooves clop
in the skies over Alabama, hallelujah! Will you
lift your hands over your head like this and raise
the roof shouting hallelujah? Hallelujah! Amen.

Can I have one more Amen? Say it loud. Open
yourself wide as the sky over Alabama. Hallelujah!
Mercy, mercy, we'll wear those blue robes
as we cross the river together, yes sir, hm-mmm.

--He found himself in his condemned apartment,
        and he took a bite of a crisp apple,
        a firm red apple, and he chewed
        and smacked his lips, yes sir, he did.

House

As you move through these rooms,
remind yourself: this is your house,
faded carpet, painted-shut window

sashes, dull knives in the cupboard.
Remind yourself that mice dwell
inside the pantry wall and dry rot

blights the front porch. Remind
yourself that the peeling front yard
fence reveals your property boundary.

Remind yourself that prior residents
polished these oak bannisters, laid
cobblestone paths, and joined joists,

studs, rails, and rafters each to each.
Remind yourself that ancestors laid
stone upon stone and set this copper

weathercock upon the roof's ridge.
Remind yourself that a master
gardener cultivated the climbing

roses embellishing the garden arch,
and a predecessor excavated this fish-
pond and stocked it with dappled

koi. Mind you, near the abandoned
depot the two-lane blacktop ends.
You will find an unplowed field

that converges with prairieland
where blue night unfolds. A wolf
moon traces an archway you cross

where silence settles on thistles
and grasses, a space so quiet
it surpasses understanding. Remind

yourself that one day in leaving
through the garden gate you will,
beyond understanding, not return.

Howdy, Partner

Wary of the masked jester who
shadows me, I whistle as if nothing's
amiss. No, I am not dreaming
because I'm awake, aren't I?

Adding to confusion, I don't know
how, lacking a winter coat or warm
galoshes, I arrived here walking
along these railroad tracks, snow falling.

The masked clown must be demonic,
red nose and diabolical smile. God,
whenever I snap my head round—
like this— the fool ducks away,

not allowing me to confront him
because truth must trump falsehood.
I swear I'll pull off his artificial face,
and sucker punch his powdered jowls

until he howls for mercy. As snow
thickens, I wade knee-deep, plodding
ahead not knowing where I'm going
or when the rascal will accost me.

Aren't clowns annoying? When he
draws near, I'll pivot and grab hold
of his faux face, which will release
like a champaign cork. "Beg pardon,"

I'll say, "Just who the hell do you think
you are?" Finally, we'll be nose to nose,
assessing each other, and we'll discover
we are identical, north and south poles

of the same planet, and so, amazed,
our eyes shall widen in recognition.
Embracing like long-lost brothers,
we'll laugh and laugh and cry and cry.

VIII.

Gathering

Ah, here they are, silent ones
gathering like choristers. Many I
haven't seen in decades, but lately

wherever I go they materialize like
ice-sheathed exhalations. Recognizing
faces, I know they are dead, yet here

they are poised to sing melismatic scales.
I see them, pentimento aspects, chins
up, waiting for a conductor's downbeat.

At the dog park, I notice canine sidekicks
for whom I tossed tennis balls. I see
them chasing rabbits into blackberry

briers. They heel and howl before leaping
for frisbees. At the ballpark, the radio
announcer raises his voice, "That ball

is going, going, way outta here." We stand
and cheer, familiar faces fading behind me
all the way to the last grandstand row where

my late father scans the outfield with high-
powered German binoculars, adjusting
the thumb dial, zooming to the batter circling

bases, to skyrockets exploding over the fence,
to hometown players spilling from their dugout —
before lowering the huge lenses squarely

toward me, my hand extending as if to receive
a toss, as if I shall catch this pitch and not let it
fall this time, not this time, not ever again.

Doppelgänger

1

Sonoran Desert, noon,
crossing an arroyo, I see
a heat-warped silhouette,
a mirage, opening its arms to me,
before dissolving in glaring light.

2

"Pardon me," I say. "Have we met?"
Opposite ends of a park bench,
we watch two black swans skim
across the pond. Their grisly red
eyes burrowed above a float of feathers.

3

Someone's pacing the plank
flooring in the apartment
above as my heart beats
in synchrony to each footfall,
beat for beat, step for step.

4

Before dawn, I wake as a train
shrieks and soon rattles
over the trestle near town,
my bedroom window clattering.
Remembrances of my father.

5

Crows cawing on the chimney
cap as dogwood branches brush
the cedar siding that my father
stained the year before he died.
I hear a peacock scream.

6

Bedroom light across the street
dims before the house darkens.
I see a familiar figure, my size,
framed in the dark window.
We stare at each other.

7

Two a.m., I finger my receding
hairline in the bathroom mirror
and am reminded of my father,
how he would brush his silver hair.
Oh, my father. Oh, my father!

My Last Lecture

Members of the Academic Excellence Committee,
faculty, staff, and students: Imagine your dog's legs
become paralyzed, so you jury-rig a pantyhose sling

which allows you to lift him to the lawn where,
suspended, he hovers and can eliminate excreta
before lying by the picket fence where he may sniff

and interpret neighborhood scents. Imagine waking
at night to comfort him as his atrophied legs drum
against the floor. Imagine your need for coherence,

for purpose beyond words. To be clear, my lectures
offered from this dais were often academic, and, I fear,
their substance and subtexts merely feathers and crumbs,

except for the example I just mentioned, the support
for your dog friend, the one whose heft you bear
because you adore the body and blood of him. Also,

imagine a set of scales, weight and counterweight,
stability of galaxies, gravity and inertia keeping,
mystifyingly, the firmament in sync, equilibrium

of sun, planets, moons, comets — centrifugal forces
swinging in supportable orbit, this authority holding
us in its sling, keeping us balanced, and refusing to let go.

River

This river runs
into an estuary where
we float on currents
and bathe in blue light.

Adrift, we encounter
confluences, waves
and wind channeling us
on our brief passage.

Rivers within us spill
into an unfathomable
sea, to depths where
we must go together.

IX.

Wind Telephone

Installed in the garden parterre
a phonebooth shelters a rotary phone
that has no dial tone because the handset is detached.
A laminated note describes how to use

the rotary phone in the phonebooth,
though, of course, the handset receives no dial tone.
The note encourages visitors to call
a disconnected dear one no longer alive,

though, of course, the handset's detached —
the dialed number no longer in service —
so topiary hedges finally reflect the caller's voice.
The finger-wheel clack-clicks as it spins,

dialing a number no longer in service.
Even so, the caller senses a removed presence.
The metal finger-wheel click-clacks as it spins,
but only a whisper of wind rustles through the line

between the caller and a distant shore.
Eventually the caller says what should have been
said long ago but hears only a whisper of wind,
an echo across the gap above the wide river.

Prayer or confession, what was left unsaid
enters the detached handset with no dial tone.
Words echo over the gap of the wide river,
far from the garden parterre phonebooth.

Waiting Room

As you press a hand to the wound,
the full-length mirror reflects your pain.
Musak speakers hiss. The furnace sighs.

You study the black-and-white Life
magazine covers above a lone Angelfish,
fins and gills toiling to keep life hovering

over turquoise aquarium gravel. Panic-
stricken, you notice the room has no doors,
only walls and that large looking glass — how,

you wonder, did you enter this room?
An electric eye blinks. You may be losing
your mind. When light starts to fade, you

lean forward and ask aloud, "What's going
on, anyway?" Once the speakers fall silent,
you sense someone will appear, so you sit

still and wait, refusing to shut your eyes
as memory slips into twilight. Cartoons
at the Grand Illusion, matinee Saturday:

while credits rolled and ushers swept popcorn
between aisles, your mother gripped your hand
and led you from theater comforts straight

into stunning light, snow falling. Blinding
and loud, outside frightened, and you wished
to stay in the sanctuary of cinema's dark

enchantment. With age, though, you left fear
behind and found gifts of sunbursts and breathed
deeply the air of mountain meadows. You

found silence in Gothic cathedrals, and watched
snow piling against the weatherside of the house,
marveled at night sky above Montana and barns

filled with the smell of horses and hay,
sourdough bread rising on sunlit windowsills,
hummingbirds dipping their tiny bills in flutes

of honeysuckles. Now, even though you linger
in this room with an Angelfish encased in
an aquarium and treading water, each moment

becomes an interlude, a solitude as you watch
images grow and then fade in the mirror,
abstract shapes shifting like lava lamp blobs.

You get used to the twilight and feel a kinship
with the Angelfish as it treads water, its jaws
and lips opening and closing like a heart valve.

Hole

Leaning over the edge, you sense
the gravitational tug. Attracted
and repelled, you circle it. You

drop a penny into it and wait....
The thought of falling takes
your breath away, doesn't it?

As they convene to dictate safety
guidelines, authorities avow, "Holes
must be covered." They also post

a warning: "It is forbidden to enter
or to modify this hole." If you
curse into its throat, your voice

echoes its own response. After all,
a hole is what's missing, isn't it?
Approaching its emptiness, silence

greets you. No wonder when you
gaze into its depth, you imagine
water pearling over stone-filled creeks.

Like fireflies, memories flash and burn
through space as you lean over the brink
and stare into the reflection of a starless

sky. You see water filling the hull
of a broken boat, smoke curling
from a bedroom window, and chicken

hatchlings peeping, oblivious of a gray rat
snake's tongue tasting the air and drawing
near. Back to sky, you say a prayer

like tossing a coin into a wishing well,
like squinting at unbearable light,
like falling without hitting bottom.

Closed Campus

Acres of deserted parking spaces except
for one police car, driver side door open,

no officer in view. Bomb scare?
Power outage? Welcome Center locked—

no note. You cup your hands to the glass
door, an empty foyer. No students stroll

across the quad where cherry blossoms
pose in splendor. You hurry to the dorms

and say, "No one." A cosmic prank?
You try library entrances and scan

footpaths leading to upper campus
and to the Gothic arches. The obelisk

radiates loneliness. No planes drone
across the sky, and no traffic whispers

from border roads ringing the campus.
Even crows, pigeons, and squirrels are gone.

You jog toward the stadium. Perhaps
an evacuation drill? You mutter, "What

on earth?" Jumping the turnstile, you
hurry onto the AstroTurf Field and discover

nothing but a drum major's hat. Breathing
heavily, you head toward the arboretum,

shuffling through leaf shadows and green
hollows, among hedges and leafy boughs.

No one. No one. Arriving at the lakeshore —
no boats, ducks, geese, seagulls — green

algae curdled on water's surface. If only
you could find one witness. Just one.

On the roped-off lifeguard tower a sign
warns, "Swim at your own risk." You

climb the ladder and assume the elevated
chair. You imagine a swimmer calling

for help beneath the diving board,
a boy about to drown, a life you might

save if you knew how to swim. "Is there no
one here, no one anywhere?" What good

is a story without an audience? Unbearably
alone, you realize today is yet another day.

Dog

—at the parking pull-off near Ruby Beach,
north coast Washington state

Screaming curses, the driver yanked
open the passenger door and pulled
the Golden Retriever by its collar,

hurling the animal to the ground
before kicking it in the ribs.
Standing over the yelping creature,

the driver emptied his rage, stomped
to his rumbling Jeep, and then sped
away, tires pelting gravel and dust.

Save us, the dog, to make amends
or whatever governs devotion in dogs,
hurtled down Highway 101, chasing

the man who assaulted it. Nothing
could stop it, nor its duty to atone
as it dashed along the center stripe

of the blacktop road. Panting hard,
it shall run as its battered heart allows.
It shall run and run, no matter what.

Oh, No!

Why yes, we did hear night screams
and sirens, peoples' lives in crisis.
Since you asked, we've always lived

in well-lit homes, doors deadbolted.
For good measure, we've repeated
our creeds and surely been forgiven.

Midnight, doorbell buzzes and two
cops on the stoop. One says, "Excuse
us. May we come in?" The other says,

"You may want to sit down." "Oh, no,"
we say, "what happened?" Showing us
a blurry photo, one asks, "Do you

know this man?" The man in the photo
looks familiar, so we say, "Looks familiar."
They say, "We have a few questions."

"Oh, no," we say, "what is going on?"
"Like everyone," they say, "you're
about to find out." "Oh, no," we say,

"there must be some mistake."
One says, "That's why we're here,
mistakes. It's our job to fix mistakes."

"Oh, no," we say, "what do you want
with us?" "That's what we are here
to find out." "Find what?" They say,

"You may want to call a lawyer."
"What? Why?" "When people make
mistakes they usually need lawyers."

"Oh, no! Are we in trouble?"
"That's really the point of our visit."
How long has it been since they

insinuated themselves into our living
room? Finally we hint, "Thanks for stopping
by. Wish we could have been more helpful."

They appraise us from the comfort
of our Ikea couch and ask, "You don't
understand why we're here, do you?

Shall we start from the beginning?"
"Oh, no!" Hours pass, and then we
admit, "We all make mistakes, right?"

They say, "Yeah, we know all about it.
Shall we get all this in writing?" We say,
"Oh, No! But we didn't mean harm."

Speaking Metaphorically

Our train stops half a day from the depot,
high desert. Ordered to disembark,
we hear eerie night sounds, hoof beats

and screeching night birds swooping
so close we feel the air feathering our
cheeks. Desert voices, too, peeping

and clicking near enough to touch.
Afraid we might disturb a diamondback
or step on a jumping spider nest, we

move warily. One of our party weeps.
Others moan. "We'll all die. No one knows
we're here." We no longer stay together

but trudge ahead in small cliques. When
someone dies, we frame the body with sun-
bleached stones and leave before outspread

wings descend. Mornings reveal a red
scar, horizon blazing like an infection.
Why, we wonder, did the conductor leave

us here? Unexpectantly, we reach a slow-
moving river, alluvial bottomland ordaining
the other shore. Salvation, fellow travelers,

for we hear laughter rising above treetops
on the other side. We know we must cross
over. When a skiff appears, we crowd

the riverbank and watch a coxswain push-
poling slowly toward us before transporting
us across one at a time. We face forward

as the boat rocks and water laps the keel.
Behind us the steerer hums a melody. We
mouth the words but make no sound.

Winter Light

Blue highlights in her hair, she
plucks a guitar, sings to a sinking
man whose lips open and close

like a fish's mouth. Door ajar, first
room on the left, she sings, "Don't
worry. Be happy." During the refrain,

he lip-synchs the words. Singer
and patient face winter light glazing
the hospice window. Doesn't joy

flow like a river, its current easing
into a blue lagoon? Have you felt
the enchantment of a frozen meadow?

Player and patient grin as they
hum because they have discarded
lyrics — merely music remains.

Stephen Jaech is grateful to the editors of the
following publications where some of these
poems first appeared.

Poetry Northwest
College English
Porch
Christian Science Monitor
Seattle Review
Four Zoas Press

STEPHEN JAECH'S poems have appeared in *College English, Poetry Northwest, Seattle Review, The Christian Science Monitor,* among many other publications. As an award-winning writer and college educator, his publications include two chapbooks "Many Rooms" and "The Machine that Destroys Itself" in addition to a novel, *King of Crows.* He served as a guest columnist for the *News Tribune* and was included in the Washington Commission for the Humanities Inquiring Minds panel of speakers. Now retired from Pierce College, he lives in Steilacoom, Washington with his partner Kathrina.

www.ingramcontent.com/pod-product-compliance
Lightning Source LLC
Chambersburg PA
CBHW020417130626
46549CB00006B/2602